A Landscape to Figure ...

A LANDSCAPE TO FIGURE IN

Poems

Helen Boden

RED SQUIRREL PRESS

First published in 2021 by Red Squirrel Press
36 Elphinstone Crescent
Biggar
South Lanarkshire
ML12 6GU
www.redsquirrelpress.com

Edited by Elizabeth Rimmer

Layout, design and typesetting by Gerry Cambridge
e:gerry.cambridge@btinternet.com

A CIP catalogue record for this book is available from the
British Library.

ISBN: 978 1 913632 23 6

Red Squirrel Press is committed to a sustainable future.
This publication is printed in the UK by Imprint Digital
using Forest Stewardship Council certified paper.
www.digital.imprint.co.uk

Contents

FLEET

Horse chestnut leaves
out across the road:
Hillend disappears

Valley Town

Streets lineate the hillside,
terrace above the A-road and river.
Houses, built for workers
in whatever line went on
because of the watercourse,
and caused the arterial road,
look down on industry's
light inheritors of the valley bottom:
carparks, units, retail parks.

Millennial development has improved
on flats put up on the hill
in the sixties: balconies
with better prospects,
wood / glass walkways that bridge the slope.

The cemetery at the end
of the one bisecting lane
is half-way up onto the moor
that keeps town at bay,
that rebuffs by night
mill-shop, golf course, holiday home,
the shadow of the valley; that
is darker than the unpolluted sky.

Emley Moor

Mast: slender against the horizontals' sway,
beacon to the valley dweller, textile worker,
homing student, her. *See both coasts*
from the top on a clear day. Old folks say
the direction of weather overhead
—or maybe it's the colour of the clouds—
can predict election winners.
Or Derby winners. Either way, it signals more
than gameshows, chat shows, local news.

From an Upper Window

When I glance up the weather's changed.

A flecked veneer,
a liquid map of fallen rain
clings onto the velux pane
whose obscured aspect no longer
frames the altering pattern of light and tide.
The glass has become an Ordnance Survey sheet,
an entirely scree-pocked three-foot square,
an image of the psoriasis-surface
of weathered rock viewed at a distance
like that from here across the loch.

Fluent

Light ripples dark lines of calligraphy onto waves at Clubbiedean.
It looks to us like Arabic.
Messages flow by, replaced
by a similar script saying something else
while the original moves on
                    a syllable less
                              a sound compressed
towards the anglers' caravan on the man-made bank.
While light remains the same and wind is constant
the meniscus repeats its hand. Redrafts.

Water levels low / Cloud levels may vary / Return all brown trout!

By the time we've finished eating snacks the words
have merged into something like a moving typeface.
When we try to decipher this freshwater autocue
we can only come up with an aquatic transcription
of the imperatives tacked to the boundary fence:

ZAKAZ LOWIENIA.   TEREN PRYWATNWY!
*Przejmie prosi sie o nie korzystanie tego miejsca—teren zarezerwowany**

We ask the man at the caravan
if he can tell us what the notices say.
He explains about confusion
between subsistence and sport,
and offers to put the kettle on.

After some riffing on recently changed implications
                    wider insinuations
                          the small print
                                    messages getting across

I revert to wondering
if the wind dictates the words,
or reads what's relayed up from mass
and weight of water underneath,
as arbitrary sign of atmospheric mood,
no projection of ours at all,
the way you can see the phrenology of tide
in the marks it leaves in sand;
or warps and folds in weathered rock remain
as pattern, contour lines: a relief map of its own terrain.

Fishing Prohibited / Private Land /
You are asked not to use this place—it is reserved ground

Sign

—After Fernand Léger

He came upon   an abandoned farm
near Montréal,
a *SLOW* sign warped
around a tree trunk
spoke and hub and axle
of impacted vehicle
embedded in the letters so they said
US LOVE or *U.S. LOVE,*
Vs. LOVE, or *WW2*

He came back
to paint the junk and overgrowth:
moved around the prongs
that made the letters up.
Cubist-clever, planetary,
re-articulated
SLOW

We look back   and re-arrange.
By repetition, permutation, see
in an abandoned farm near Montréal,
a tractor left to rust in Uist;
hope that if we can't right
that boy-racer crash
by spooling back
erasing the track
to the moment preceding
the veer on the bend at the reservoir,
then at least we can save
some roadkill or a stricken seabird...

Scores on rough ground   turn
into route-maps to when
long-haired, in knee-high grasses,
we ran, receding
                    speeded up

Migrant

Faith will have stitched herself into this cityscape
by the time her Robin's fledged, leaves for study
in London or visits his grandpa in Zimbabwe,
and she squeezes that plaid bird she ran up for his first Christmas
into a suitcase he's chosen to pack. He won't remember
what it's like to have no choice but Faith won't
let him forget. No matter he's not so keen on soft toys now,
he and that home-made bird will fly to Harare, to where
the sub-saharan sea eagle, stylised in soapstone, became
a national emblem. He'll learn of its origins
and his other history.

                         One day he'll be back,
still with that trinket in his hand luggage, fraying a bit, alongside
stamps and coins embossed with the Bateleur. He'll pass them all on
to his own bairns, born to recognise the northern species' song
and know cold Christmases and why their father's namesake's
breast is red. Faith will reminisce for them, tell
of the first December; how she fashioned a tartan robin
to occupy her hand, distract her mind, give herself something
to give her four-year-old son.

Litmus

Jayne didn't know not to prune
hydrangeas when they faded.
The first spring her Matty didn't see
the bush under their front window
failed to flower. By then the house
was up for sale. Come autumn
she was down in Shropshire, nearer
to Maddie, John and other kin.

Jayne learned from her new neighbour,
Joan, how the colour they bloom
depends on whether the earth is acidic.
Forever Pink has as much a chance
of coming up azure as Nikko Blue,
and Everlasting Amethyst could turn out
sapphire. How hard it can be to adapt the soil,
especially so close to a concrete path.

Not the Territory

—Covenanter's Grave, Pentland Hills

His July-warmed headstone's red
facing Bleak Law and Darlees Rig.
Beyond the col connecting them
turbines tilt the Ayrshire skyline.

You come up here
more to commemorate
Adam Sanderson, shepherd of Blackhill,
who knew the place to inter
the body of the man whose dying wish
he'd chosen to respect

> than for the anonymised insurgent,
> who fled (he limped) from Rullion Green
> in the direction of home.
> Made it as far as Sanderson's.

Ascending with your Vibram soles
daysac, Windstopper fleece,
you're here to wonder how the hill man
bore the rebel's body
between
the shutter-speed of seasons
to bury him in sight of his home.

You walk in from the road
for what the maps can't show
of gradient   up-rising
ditch concealed in heather
depth of cleugh   conventicle site
extent of ruin   vegetation height

—how land lies—

for that first southwest sight-line.

All this
and how your pace will change
pursued by clouds and a following wind
on the way back to the pub:
what the track feels like underfoot.
The variation in the pink of its tint.

Young Buck

—After Colin Blanchard

in his shadow he's cast his own lore
self-portrait as a landscape

I am   Actaeon

the Capelaw beast
under whose branchy legs
corrugated grasses sing
syllables
                    fleet
                              gone
narrow-backed
he can't project
more than a pentameter or two
before the wind
startles
still life to movie
ceramic-set
he's fixed on ninety paces hence
at some moorside mottling
he smells
                    he knows
is beak and tail
of what a raptor let remain
gaze
          ears
                    nostrils
pegged
on metaphor
for chase and prey
rejection

      kill
he faces the
symbolism of
the *cervidae*
innards spilled
in consonants and vowels
these days when
he sees
motorway deer-signs
start to outnumber deer

Young Mortality

(i) *Monumental Mason, Uist*

In every graveyard on the seaboard
He stoops through a 21stC summer
Repairs what winter's undone
Figures into stones beyond
Preservative peat, on shores
Eases back the sands
Re-engraving, saving
The recovered from sea
From perpetual deluge
From further erasure

(ii) *Kirkibost*

'I'm just enjoying the humidity', said the Bernera fisherman, sitting with
a drink outside his house. He inevitably knew a Sutherland fisherman I
once knew, and told me tales of the lightning across Loch Roag last night;
of their purchase many years ago of a motor vehicle from Badnabay, and
finding the most direct route to a licensed premises, amphibian across the
shallows of the head of Loch Laxford. So characteristic, I thought, and I
recalled a shared dram in the Sound of Handa. It hadn't occurred to me
that humidity was something to be enjoyed, though our mutual friend
Alasdair, who had similarly relished his own front-door view, towards
Stoer, might also have said this when he was still alive on the other side of
the Minch.

Sir Walter Scott's *Old Mortality* is named for the man who tended and
repaired the inscriptions on memorials to the Covenanters, the 'persecuted
Presbyterians' of the seventeenth century, in rural churchyards.

This poem is dedicated to families who have lost multiple members at sea.

In Suburbia (i): In Praise of Blossom

A sudden greening makes the park opaque
against its backdrop of brick or air
and you, the roadside show pony, can go to town
imparting a pink flavour to our afternoons again.

We turn a corner and our own suburb
could be in Amsterdam or Arles.
Five trees beside St Peter's become
our fresh point of pilgrimage. We pace across
the playing field into the wind to where
contortions of *prunus* have begun to defy
gravity and ladle up soft garlands to propitiate a sky
that glows bright and warm in sympathy
yet will not really reckon them or spare beyond
a three-week carnival and one 4am squall.

But for now we are privileged as distinguished guests
to walk under and look up through these festoons, fairground-
dizzied by clumps and clusters pom-pommed to cheer
in the short season at the end
of each branch's prevailing reach.

Flesh, and Blood

'I regard atopic eczema as a disease of two or more people'
—Ted Grossbart

She'd make you promise
no more secrets (what about hers?)
so you scoured truths
on arms rough and branchy
as birch-bark manuscript.
Embossed your reality on a nonlinguistic skin.

Kept mum.

Scratched out instead what could not be said
on torso and limbs
not syntactical lines or alphabet
but encrypted, more like punctu-
ation marks or code (you'd learned
the need to protect your data).
Better to make yourself illegible—
having three foreign languages, excelling in physics,
wasn't enough to create a safe distance.

(See here, the deep history of yourself:
a read-through denial, gainsaying,
of all those accusations,
the *Don't Contradicts*
the *Settle Downs.*
A refusal to calm
flesh that would not keep silence.)

Incompetent embroidery,
you were tacked to yourself
by the underground protest

of articulate dermis:
mingle of layers,
muddle of connective tissue,
a mixing-up of flesh and blood
pin-prick pierced the surface.
Erupted, warped, folded,
too unlike the sedimentary
better-to-replenish function of a *normal* skin.

On the surface you lived
like a grotesque sculpture,
improvised performance piece.
Tired of being told *Pull yourself together*
you'd make the best
of the material you'd been given.
Start from scratch.
Make an exhibition of yourself.

Will Not Be Prosecuted

What of the childish incursions, pushing
in the tuckshop queue, sneaking a peek
at presents on top of grandma's wardrobe

trying to breed mice in a neighbour's outhouse
breaking into public buildings after hours
setting a fire on the playing field

chased off the golf course
next door's garden have a good look (don't touch)
refused entry to _____

Climbing walls, you were the one
unsure you should be here at all: Lynn Shaw
had conviction, she once stole a bench.

Later, you learned of the worthy ones, mass moves
for open access: Kinder Scout, holes
in perimeter fences. Pushing boundaries,

of course it felt like you were the one
being trespassed against. All those
inoculations, dentists. First smear test.

Legislations followed to protect
walkers' rights, but what of your parents'
decreasing mobility.

Security-cams can follow your kids,
can't prevent scanning of horizons.
What of all that traffic urging

into country lanes, hi-vized officials
who gatekeep the national park.
In the cows' field, farmer

and Right of Way sign both say it's ok
to go through but the occupants
are blocking the exit gate.

Your puddled indent seeps into theirs,
channels back along the riverside path,
your north side to the mountain, moored.

The 'mass trespass' of Kinder Scout, Derbyshire, in
1932 protested against the restricted access of walkers
and city workers to privately owned land. It is credited
with leading to legislation to establish national parks
and long-distance footpaths.

Beyond the Blunt End of the Capelaw Plateau

Venus descends, as if with care, barely above
the outline of the lower slope, an easy incline
with which it can trace a common gradient,
and seem to levitate a human's height above
like the torch of a benighted walker or ranger

steadying their way off the hill—as though,
like a decelerated version of the runner
who came off the summit at the weekend when
I was climbing up, it were actually advancing,
north, towards our homes down here, where
its action and the darkening of the ridge happen

on the retina. I sit and watch the hill lose light
in two dimensions, as on every unclouded night
I'm in, and the star that contours its descent.
It matters that my feet know how it is to tread
up there at 6am in June, dewed boot rising from
grass-pad grace note to scree-kick diphthong or

carolling a ringing track, then trudging into westerlies,
hair wind-chilled onto January cheeks. I'd turn
to face back down here and single out my own
front door, anchored by the moor's breadth,
while the planet that plotted such a similar course
over this hill in autumn set elsewhere.

PROOF

Here at the edge of the firth you can
start to feel the curvature of the earth

The Gallery Tour Pauses in Front
of Simon Armitage's Portrait

—After Paul Wright, 'Simon Armitage',
and Simon Armitage, 'Strike Two'

Smudged askance, we can't decide
if he's looking at himself,
already looking back, at twenty-eight
writing how he liked his filling-out of face—
or at what scenery seems to be behind,
the landscape he's to figure in.

Even as his dyke-wide shoulders
are rising, darkly, out of snow
he's thinking Marsden Caribbean,
lilac-lushened. Turquoise splashed
in verticals falls to make paradisical
pools of the Huddersfield canal.
Even what appears up-close
as the sage of Pennine grass
with grit-stone underlay
is turned tropical by a three-hour sitting.

Painter's abstractions of geology, weather,
defy an easy correspondence
with the fault-lines of the poet's face,
behind which he might be thinking
of war zones, famine, stuff
he mustn't forget to pick up on the way home
or, to pass the time while posing,
fixing a stanza, working out a line.

This painted smile's more rueful
than the one he verbalized

a couple of decades before.
Whatever's behind him,
jungle—indiscretion—moor
could stand for what's behind us all.

We read his words in front of him,
imagining some movement
by the corner of his lips,
sure he's just about to clear his throat.

Kinlochbervie

—After John Bellany

(i)

Here is land's last stand against the Atlantic.
The defiance of the limb it flexes out!
—muscular, as animate
as those human forms reluctant
who reappear to prophesy
their sons' returning to the element:
kin, locked in genetic concatenation
between gneiss and shore, in a frieze
of lives lived short and hard on the edge
of the channel's slim refuge from the ocean,
before Wrath turns gentle, prosperous, Orcadian.

(ii)

Unsung now the fishing's gone
thirty years after John Bellany
painted the port's biblical stasis

everything's empty: ice-factory,
warehouses. Carpark's empty
of the people-carriers that bussed

across fishers from the east to work
the KLB boats in the nineties—
where, pinned against the Mission
by a force eight, you could
witness the northern lights.

Eardley

the grass stalks and seedheads she collaged onto fieldscapes
that people thought would wither
                                        still there six decades after
she dared
            to live on the edge
took these hard conditions for herself   chose extremes

Townhead's back streets
last house on the clifftop at Catterline
                                    with bare earth floor   no mains
basic conditions
                    not so different from each other

already making more from sales
than what she wanted
for purchase of oils
boat-paint
hardboard—more robust
than canvas on the north-east coast—
some food
train ticket

                                for the commute from Glasgow
scooter
        left at Stonehaven station
for a month up at Catterline
                                weeks back in Townhead

for five years until she switched
around her subject and viewpoint   turned
from the fields and watch-house to where
village bordered on the sea:

its stony beach
salmon nets

                                    what was beyond

she'd have a series: a dozen works
from / of the same location
in progress at any one time
continue with whichever one
suited the day's conditions best
what the weather most resembled
when she was out there last

when approaching blizzards sent
fishermen
back into the salmon bothy

                                    she went out to paint
the storm
                        freehand
—less time now for sketches
to be refined in the studio—
put the atmosphere   like those grasses
directly into her work
caught the wave that breached
the harbour wall

clifftop cottage   innercity tenement
                                    both condemned

these the reconfigured forms she bequeathed
this her tempest   her winter's tale

Collagrapher

—After Rosemary Bassett

Strolling
>   print-making

she beachcombs the flotsam at dawn
>   —today a netting offcut

sifts the morning catch for what to save
>   sees what it tells her

fishwife-fretting
>   repairs a few of the holes

trusts her medium
to sluice out
detritus of resentments

fixed
>   with yacht varnish
>   it dries like bladderwrack
>   seawall cobblestone
>   ancient map

inked up
>   a billow of fabulous scale

in an armslength / wingspan frame: collagraph seamonster
>   familiar amphibian
patrols her living room

wideangled

        a coastal epidermis

                suggestion of tide

Collagraphy is a printmaking process where objects are fixed
(collaged) onto a board prior to inking.

The Only Way She's Her Father's Daughter

With no one to meet me
at Ribblehead Station
I carry on a stop to Horton,
climb Pen y Ghent
pilgrimaging the footfall of my father
who shouldered his pushbike
over these peaks
before marriage and daughter
or Goretex and knobbly tyres.

Walkers bound across ice-encrusted bogs
uncrossable without detour most days of the year.
At the summit they bond
beyond the proprietary hail.
But 'where do you come from?'
is a tricky one to respond to here,
impossible to answer now.
Edinburgh?
'Nice. But you don't sound Scottish.'
The West Riding, then?
'Oh, so does my father-in-law. Whereabouts exactly?'
Dewsbury? Child neglect and racial tension?
On the edge of the Pennines?
In the foothills "   "   "
if my inquisitor has a lyric look?
Or even: *I went to the same school*
as Barbara Hepworth?
Between Leeds and Huddersfield sounds too mundane
and often elicits that deflating demand
for greater specificity.
'My mum was from
a village called Thornhill', I say.
At the bottom of Horton Scar Lane

no one's waiting in the Pen y Ghent Café.
I chat with some mountain bikers
over pints of tea and a Chorley cake
about eclectic place-names
                              calorific intake
                                        the depths to which our tracks embed.

Some Seascapes

—After Emily Learmont

(i) *Graphic*

an inkblot cloud pursues the boats
like a speech bubble
flurries of vowels   morphemes   ideas
on a punctuation-flecked sea

swirls   whorls
of inverted commas
conversation billows
between the fleet

a thought detaches   memory sprays
                a wake for the clearances

will they consolidate
into a skerry of memory?

night   nautical twilight   civil twilight   day
             calm   storm   calm   storm   calm

plot the sound

I saw three. . .

(ii) *Isthmus*

Skeletal-chalked—
fine lines of rigging
fresh-vein the moon

(iii) *Clearance*

Ship parts the coasts
of Knoydart   Sleat
like a centrifugal force

funnels thought

when the storm has passed
through the vessel

is that a second ship
or *fata morgana*
the soul of the boat
or its counterpart
inverted on the horizon
beyond   the end of the sound

is the ship   or weather
fugitive—
one vessel the other's unconscious   or ours

ship drops anchor in the sound
sets a lantern
a thousand onshore lights
glow back   as the darkest hour departs

departs   for Carolina

leaves a filigree wake
                              a waning moon

a morning sun like marbled paper

Glaister-Rime

Late January   flank of Capelaw
we rest   at the gatepost that plays
the Prelude to *Tannhauser*
in certain southwesterlies

can't find   a word
for underfoot freeze-thaw-freeze

that makes muscle-ache ascent   on days
of local brightness   when no wind tunes that gate
on the Pentlands   no Fife
no Ochil   other side of firth

just the sails of the new bridge
floating   the haar

The Play's the Thing

Szemünk pillás függönye fent: / Hol a szinpad: kint-e vagy bent, / Urak, asszonyságok?
The curtain of our eyelids is raised: / Where is the stage, outside or within, / Ladies and gentlemen?

—Bartok, *Bluebeard's Castle*, Prologue

Only when the orchestra beats
on the same frequency as our hearts
do we remember how to forget

across pits lit like the night-decks of ships
—takes a whole day to turn them around
Volta, Da capo—

how behind some slant prosceniums
the wrong sides of the balustrades
draft soliloquies were touched up

by actors, forming themselves out of
inklings first, then words designed
to avoid their own inferno, Tartarus.

Play of light on the back-cloth
can never emulsion over their
self-hate, their overgrown nails.

In Suburbia (ii): Ways of Looking at Blossom

across the park   a blushing smudge

middle-distance   in the pink

closer up   dense hooflike buds

under   a calligraphy of arthritic gnarl

from a sixth storey window   magenta dread-locked mop

stravaigin   on an evening circumambulation

sugar-candy coated   from the inside out

systematically   *Prunus cerasifera*

comprehensively   every stereotype you can recall in five breaths

tangentially   in a station of the métro

in the National Gallery   tourists survey symbolic impasto

on Google   a forest

carpet   on the pavement following a May hurricane

floating   on the Union Canal, only Ophelia absent

Oxgangs to Abruzzo

—After Robbie Bushe

on the fault-line
between Firrhill and Pescara
in the fissure
of the Adriatic and Mains Drive
open border

where memory is highway
minor roads pursue inclines

the way suburban sheds pitch up at the shore
& beach huts can alight on someone's lawn

Appenine and Pentland cleft
for exodus and influx
across a rift
invite continuing pursuit, flight
direct, return, dreich to light

Vernacular

the assimilated ones   framed
in shed doorways
like portraits of their proprietors
we watch   are heard
under the apexes
where we set up our ancestry
as figureheads
familiars
to ward off
        the next wave
            to pose a threat

our hinterlands are arrayed inside

            lock / unlock   now our choice

we stronghold the archive of the time
when they didn't believe it wasn't us
who stole the necklaces
pin up our oboe certificates
the paraphernalia of winning   being picked first

          unlock / lock
          though between cracks
          memories oxidise

it hinges on this
        the compassion
of our gatekeeping
readiness to share
refuge

approach now
        shelter

The Museum Labels Are Liturgical

By the grace of the Archangel
they say
all those messages in bottles
that wash up in the bay
are miracles
        Many of these have arrived
they say one day all the plastics
in the ocean
will come ashore at Panormitis
        In the bay of the monastery

they say if you do not fulfil
a promise to St Michael
        (by the grace of the archangel)
if you don't sweep
the monastery floor
the ferry will not depart
        (many of these have arrived)
you will not get away

they say
when you break your loaf
on the hot pebble beach
or in the tamarisk shade
        (in the bay of the monastery)
your allergies will abate
if you swim beneath those perfect-crescent swoops
between the crumbling peaks
your sores will be healed
        by the grace of the Archangel

they say
the mansions with that hillside-shoreside biscuit render

are warm
the houses painted blue and white stay cool
that Airbnb has distorted the economy
the landslide two years ago that took out the school
and Eva's terrace and Ioannis' courtyard
      By the grace of the Archangel
happened in the middle of the night

the taxi driver the pharmacist the waiter
the ex-pat the guidebooks
say nothing
of the camp
at the foot of the Kali Strata
of the family being forged under a tarpaulin
a lone child reading
a young woman demonstrating
something like yoga stretches
to a makeshift class
this short stretch from Asia Minor
this dusty toe-hold on Europe

      In the bay of the monastery

      Many of these have arrived

Still, Life

At fifty-plus, you've seen enough
of yourself to know
how to pose as life-model
or Dégas-dancer.
You can make a gestural haiku,
throw a provocative pose,
be a film still in the full-length mirror
on the back of the wardrobe door,
present as a detail from a famous statue.

Chilling toes gripping carpet,
curtains closed. In this light, you can't see
which scabs are healing.
Bits of you are still familiar—it's the whole
you recognise less.

If recent photographs evidence
new forearm definition
from all that cycling you do,
thighs bulk more since the last time
you stayed somewhere with a decent mirror.
You reckon a section through them would look
like a forensic specimen on crime TV
or the swollen flesh round bone
of the Sunday roast, taken
from the fridge to reach
room temperature:
stillevens, naturs morts.

Signalling Art, Not War

—After Ciara Phillips

Fingal's had a feminist makeover,
drawn from a pattern first designed
to confuse on oceans' man-made vortices.

See the wartime swirls and stripes,
charting a line from orphism to op-art,
retro-forged onto a repurposed light-ship.

Send forth abstract signals, women!
leave the siren-stereotype onshore—
transmit delight. Transport.

Let chameleon-camouflage be for land:
at sea you cannot bewilder.
Be wilder, dazzle, stand out.

Some man will try to take the credit,
but tend the light. You will launch
two thousand ships. By night reveal the code.

Every Woman was one of a series of works developed by contemporary artists to commemorate the 'dazzle ships' of the First World War. Ciara Philips 'dazzled' the former Northern Lighthouse Board ship MV *Fingal*. edinburghartfestival.com/dazzle

Castlebay

In the church of Our Lady, Star of the Sea,
two pictorial windows: fishing scene, South;
North, angelic hosts instrumental—
iconography customised; and conventional.

This doesn't overwhelm with style and scale—
what's gained here through stained glass
is a clarity that knowledge of theology
or the history of art can start to obscure.

I'm less moved than expected by
craftsmanship depicting local practice,
more affected by how these angels,
undistinguished of their kind,

make lucid an over-familiar aesthetic,
one that made me crave vernacular
bespoke for the island culture
I'd been more minded to embrace.

Guardian Angel

if a high wire
were suspended between
                    two tower blocks
Forteviot   Castleview
would you skywalk
                    cast up your aerialist shadow
onto Alpine-polystyrene clouds

the flats' rectangular shade cast down
onto the green like gargantuan coffins

like every day isn't tightrope-walking
                    between

The Festivals

When the radio transmits a concert,
live, from the Queen's Hall
across the crags
the weather plays on
right through the heart
of Midlothian into our sitting room
with interval readings, recorded,
from stories set in places
I can watch through the window
      what I see is a night some years since now,
      a version of Maeterlinck's *The Blind*
      in a backstage space at the Festival Theatre,
      where an audience in the dark looks
      at twelve unseeing faces on a dozen TV screens,
      and hears two voices: recorded
      personalities emerge then merge.
      Speakers emit words of landscape
      —sea, island, cliff, forest, lighthouse—
      sounds hostile, threatening, to these characters
      incarcerated both from places distant,
      and near enough for the sighted to recognise.
      But for each of us, responses undirected
      by stage scenery, are our own. To me,
      the central belt constricting, islands, sea, call.
      Walking down to the Usher Hall
      for a late-night recital, I try to envision
      the distance as single-track road, a Hebridean mile.

Design

—After Paul Klee, *Threatening Snow Storm*

blueprint for rebuilding
out of the bruising

provisional etching
for the reconstruction of Dresden

prophetic minaret
to a cloud-capped ground zero

Valhalla for the godless
after flood and storm

plans on the drawing-board
prefigure each apocalypse

The Mystery of Old Lathrisk

How much
              space
between the lawn   and the gate
how to elongate
                    arrive
at a drivelength   exhale

How much
                 time
between the gate   and the lawn
that extends   from walled lane
to the verge of
              footfall

Proof

They were standing in sou'westers as though a deluge and not the day-trip boat approached, offset nicely against the ochre wash of the shore houses. Amber from the harbour lights spilled down forestairs into salmonpink pools, washed the cobbles. Or that's how it looked from across on the old quay the council hasn't maintained for a decade. One of them was carrying something heavy. He beamed. The other two appeared more expectant, set to receive. One pushed back her headgear the better to scan the horizon, and the yellow haloed behind her. The middle one bent forward and their hat was the shape of a comet and looked metallic, its seam a cross-haired target. They seemed like identical triplets or twins-and-a-cousin in oilskins; like it was the fifties, or something you just did on the second Tuesday or for a heritage re-enactment of a working-harbour generation. They were too young to know much of trafficking, either, or what gets landed in hard to access coves a few miles up the coast. I thought the one on the right looked uncomfortable in yellow. He could well have been wearing must-have brands underneath all that weatherproofing, not considering of the three of them ever going separate ways, but as old pals, tidying up ropes on some similar harbour, faces weather-polished, looking back.

MOOR

Horse chestnut leaves
fall opposite the house—
Hillend re-appears

From a Boundary

(i) *April*

The day before *Das Rheingold* from the Met,
I'm back down to clear the Yorkshire house.
New York's already in daylight-saving time
and the Ring Cycle broadcast a sign
that the end of the season isn't far away.

The cooling towers of Ferrybridge
and Fixby, giants, gods, on the ramparts
of the Riding, sentinel the land they power.
Do they beam signals to that slender transmitter
on Emley Moor, opposite, and the acolyte spire
of every parish in the basin between?
All along the verge spring flowers are out
where hail squalls and sunshine alternate.

(ii) *May*

The afternoon of *Gotterdammerung*
apple blossom's interspersed with lime
along the road that curls below The Combs,
screening the colliery from the village,
the Calder levels from the last resistant spur
of Pennine millstone grit, now greened
into somewhere I'm starting not to recognise.

I place flowers on the family graves,
photograph Overthorpe, Edge Top, Scar End.
Later, Brunnhilde makes peace with her father:
that world needs to end if it's to be reborn.
I cry, not because of her vocal grain. I shan't
listen to this opera on this radio in this house again.

Asylum

The Number 5 bus,
off towards RLS's hills of home,
slips past bad parking
charity and artisan shops
on the resurfaced A702. Between
Waitrose and the Pizza Express
with Jean Brodie quotes
on its walls: Morningside Road,
route and destination.

> In hinterlands that tessellate
> with Comiston, Craighouse, Merchiston,
> Churchhill, Blackford, Grange:
> stone villas; the salubrious
> hospital parks. Astley Ainsley,
> Royal Ed. We all know someone
> who's been in

between

> its northern boundary ruled
> by the elongated back facade of Watson's College
> and where the suburban railway
> underscores the southern end

know

> how the psychiatric-hospital mythology
> resonates through neighbourhoods
> well beyond these grounds.

The site map lacks a You Are Here.
Its Red, Green, Blue walking routes
confuse. So many dead ends

you can't get round the periphery,
have to walk on the grass,
find passages through gaps

                              between clinics, wards and units
                              —Cullen—Rivers—Fergusson—
                              on the outskirts of a city
                              knows how to commemorate.

Three centuries' mixed media:
clapboard, sandstone
balustrades and redbrick.
Repurposed and purpose-built.
High rise. Low rise. Ill-advised additions.

                              On hedge-partitioned lawns
                              of the original mansions
                              in-patients make gardens
                              and grow their own,
                              paint welcome signs promoting
                              dignity—contribution—skills
                              in free-form defiance
                              of the NHS house style
                              for Laundry, Catering, Estates.

The pathway to the orchard
has a padlocked barrier
while the site is extended with the latest newbuild.

Thaw drips from trees. It sounds like rain.
Two magpies squabble at the end of the carpark

competing with rugger calls from the Watson's playground.
Beyond the asphalt a rabbit jumps
from a camouflage of dead leaves and chippings.

Back on the main drag, the homeless woman
who sits outside *Oxfam* and always says hello,
whose name I never got round to asking, isn't there.

Edge of Edinburgh

Redford and Dreghorn: the capital's
allium capitals—it hardly counts as foraging,
when ingredients for pesto
are prolific as strimmers in the gardens
of the four-in-a-blocks across the burn.
You've taught yourself to hear
traffic on the bypass as a river in spate,
convinced yourself the noise of firearm practice
from the barracks beside the woods
comes from something more benign,
more colourful than artillery.
After all, this city needs little excuse
to stage another firework display.
And here on its periphery,
the army have their own parties,
for summer fairs and Hogmanays
and ends of tours of duty—though since
the Stade de France and Bataclan
you've thought more of reaction times:
how to tell when something isn't
entertainment, isn't background noise.

You think of Owen writing home
on admission to Craiglockhart: 'I am
just going out to get the lie of the land'—
its end-of-season ramsons dell
its training trenches above the cavalry stables.
He'd be discharged before spring came again
in the Dreghorn woodlands; he wouldn't snap
the stems of invasive, grassier, more pungent
Allium paradoxum, few-flowered leek.

Calder-Hebble Navigation

Remember that Christmas when the basin
at The Leggers froze? All the way along

the towpath to The Nelson, house-boats
crisped into, glistened from, their solid dock,

season's greetings etched by claws of stranded fowl.
Crows staged some sort of pebble curling match.

Strangeness outlasted the thaw: waterway subverts
flood plain, knows it differently from how roads

appraise the terrain. A canal tells it slant
and it doesn't have to be Panama or Suez

to be strategic. The Calder Cut steers a back route
across the shroggs. It all narrows down to here.

Shroggs, scrubby woodland (N English).

Sheds

(i)

Run back down the ginnel
between Uncle Leonard's fence
and the Addymans' wall
on grass turned to mud.
Wasn't it paved?
It always rained.

It was paved.
Remember—you fell?

Shed leaned-to, didn't it?
Yet, remember running
right round the back.
Maybe that's where grass was
and the rhubarb plot.

There's corrugated iron
like on the annex roof at school
but it was always called the 'wood hut'
and didn't have a lock
—though his tools
must've been worth a bob or two.

Interior's much clearer
but you can't go back to check.
Tidy like their houses.
A bob for a job,
a slap for your cheek.
Work-ethic implements
of a pre-war blacksmith
in what never became
his pottering shed.

Put a woodblock in the vice
—turn it, tighten it—
but, like with the school Meccano set,
you don't know what to do next
so you just undo it again.
Again.

(ii)

Unlock your shed
on a thirties scheme.
Sit in its doorway
with poetry mags
chocolate éclair
filled with foraged brambles
yunnen in enamel cup.
Behind, their old ironing board
is both potting table
and bicycle rack.
You've striped the walls:
Forget-me-not and Seagrass.
Whichever way you colour it
in one hand's a Seamus digging-pen
but you had to give up Grandpa Booth's
wooden-handled tools
—the spade you till this garden with
was bought from B&Q.

Frontal

get Sandy to retell a few tales
—not the caravans   toppling off
raised beaches
sandbanks   rising tides—
perhaps the illusion
of an upsidedown island   on a sudden horizon
or inked-up seas where kelpies taunt
the ferry's wake

late afternoon   weather
that maps call an occlusion   comes in
a smirr of suburban nets
                        not the grand-theatre drapes
that closed on us nineteen days last month

foreshore
unforms   reforms
recomposes
a *clachan*   a woodland
croft house in Applecross
whose windows out-face storms

hints at the habitation we must reach
between blunt-profile headlands
Stoer   Hoy   Clo Mhor
that maps call promontories or peninsulas or points

outwit the current
round the next *rudha*   up the sound
on trunkroad tide   deepening channel
Loch Inchard   Roag   Laxford
hints of habitation
some *Tigh na Mara* we could reach
some beach to make safe landing

coast sharpens   softens   sharpens
monochrome   tint   grey

and how those few shorelights coalesce
into a town's worth   like Sandy said
when you take off your glasses

hint of a chain pier   repeat to fade

Clachan, hamlet; *rudha*, point; *Tigh na Mara*, shore-house.

Lasting Impressions

Go away, he told her: recline
for a few months on a section of shingle
in a private *plage*.
                    To him a 'beach'
was topographical, should only stop
where headlands intervened,
not the next café, bar or restaurant.
Like moors after an enclosure act,
he'd say. Kettles and pots and
third-day bruises sprang to mind.

She knew the sort of place he meant,
where you could hire a lounger
for twenty-odd euros a day, like those
Corbusier-contraptions on the Cap,
where they'd lain side by side
like warm recumbent effigies
on a wadded tomb.
                    She'd think
of those first northern painters
of the southern light, trying
to get it right, and the two of them
beside the Bertrands' pool, behind
those eight-foot cracked clay walls
onto which the sun forced all its brawn.

What will survive of us is less, she thought,
than what got soldered onto
that desiccated pool-side.
                            I'll go:
let the heat sear out all trace of him,
just as flesh, memory-foamed, springs back.

Empties

First of Jan, affluent suburb. Stockbridge,
but it could be anywhere across the island,
in Ely, Richmond, Beauly. In place of regretting
they'd put their empties out, arranged by colour,
size, acoustic property. Scores of bottles,
neatened into a pavement installation.

Should those former containers of spirits
and wine have become aeolian and sung
in the rain of their seasonal journey from
Waitrose or Aldi, they'd have borne witness
to what happened in homes in the limbo
of the holiday, before sluggish inhabitants let

the new year in, started to move on, reluctantly:
like emergence from other innocuous absorption—
World Cup for something, general election, landmark
serial drama—that removed them from routine,
occasioned special buying in. Then they'd go out,
make art from their leftovers, half-full, begin again.

Quadrille

(i) *Geometric Shelter-Belt*

A rainless month. Permitted exercise: right-angling field-boundaries
at the village edge: a cracked and popular route, not a right of way,
through desire-pathed tree-belts, council-designated *Sloping Wooded Farm
Land*. Ninety degrees, another field-length, an isolation-dance stepped
along the riggs: drop from raised verge into ditch when someone else
approaches. Improvise a distanced *pas-de-deux*: Step aside—pause—step
in—turn. Take sides across the incised channel of a modified watercourse.
Powerline, an elevated hypotenuse, intersects overhead. High-voltage
cables graph a key diagonal to/from the capital. The power grid, the
National Grid. Pylons plot a line for the hills across the axes of the shelter
belt, the green belt, the Central Belt. Slow forward. Fire hazard grows.

(ii*) Lane*

Take an evening turn: five corners out to Dalmahoy Hill. On the dried
mud path climb through the whin up the igneous sill for the view beyond
Lothian. Five corners back to the village: along ploughed fieldside
straight—*turn*—gorse-verge above freshly audible river-incision.
Whelpside—*turn*—down, across glacial-meltwater flat, over Water of
Leith and Cock Burn, up through Glenbrook (four-part burn-song, curlew
solo). Broadleafside—*turn*—along mosswalledside, beech-hedgeside
(laburnum, rhododendron, honeysuckle wilding where big-house grounds
meet the lane). Fresh-ploughed fieldside, growing lambs alongside, echo
off the Bankhead steading wall—*turn*—down/up over the nameless
burn—*turn*—larchside—Johnsburn.

(iii) *Circumstance*

Some grids are smaller—how can we measure how constrained how
limited we are in rooms in gardens if we have them—mine's triangular—
what we learn of the perimeters of our worlds within the circumferences
of daily walking, the parameters of our interpretation of the guidelines?
Streets below tenements don't have space for all the footfall round the
block. In the peripheral field-bound farmstead, formal garden, woodside,
forestside, unpolluted broom-bloom time: with improving visibility across
this moral grey area, how high how far how long is too?

(iv) *The Cockburn-Leithhead Dance*

Country-lane discipline: swerve and greet, greet and swerve, judge and be
judged by those who don't observe the passing-protocols. Walking graphs
the increase-decrease-increase of fear, blame, compliance. Of spring.
Which broadleafs are out, and which are still in bud. The further up by
the headwaters the brighter the leaves. After the farm-lanes end, beyond
the last corner that's a curve, forest starts. Access track describes a dusty-
earthed parabola down to the riverside, swerves up to the moor. Fire risk
increases. After two months of out-and-back, localised footfall, the Leith
plateau assumes small-island quiet: Auchinoon, Corston, Dalmahoy,
Kaimes, Ravelrig, the seacliffs of an imaginable coast.

Remain Moon

Four years earlier
they gathered:
the local press, the people,
in a Yorkshire market square
to pause in civic duty
at a new statue of Joseph Priestley.

A week before the Brexit vote
they came again, the people,
and the national press
laid flowers at its base, and mourned.

By the morning after the vote
they'd already edited
short-term memory, claiming
not a shot was fired in this campaign,
giving the lie to Jo Cox's belief
that *we're far more united*
and have more in common
than things that divide us.

The Remain Moon waned over Birstall,
where my German-surnamed grandfather,
the one whose brother died in France
on midsummer day 1918,
first set up shop on the market square.

And it waned over Birmingham,
where Priestley's dissenter comrades
of the Lunar Society—scientists,
industrialists, philosophers by day,
would meet at the full moon
the safer to return to homes

from which they'd be smoked out anyway
by a popular riot condoned by an establishment
intolerant of their support
of the French revolution,
their right to celebrate the anniversary
of the fall of the Bastille.

In Suburbia (iii)

One of the first things to become familiar was the pair
of mop-haired brothers who unhurried delivered
the *Evening News* to the old man opposite
in their school clothes and sneakers around 5 o' clock
sack straps across their left shoulders and fluorescent
under their right arms they would walk calmly up
his path and down again then turn right off the Drive
out of sight round the back along the Green and the Grove
before re-appearing on the bridge down the vennel
disappearing onto the Loan.
                                   It was cheering to see them
through that first sad summer then the turning back
of the clocks and the heavy snows and first spring here.
Sometime before the second winter the smaller boy was gone
and his brother already a close-cropped young man
did the paper round on his own at the same pace.
Next season the old man stopped cutting his own lawn
one of his neighbours went into residential care the other side
had a second child by which time it was easier to home in
on the best places for ramsons
                                   blossom
                                             brambles
                                                       autumn leaves.

Haar, St Michael & All Angels

ground is air is earth
is mist is soil is
light is loam is haze
is bone is breath is
foot is voice is lung

is home to their remains
their flesh made word
beneath names and dates
fixed on york stone

About the author

Writer, educator and editor Helen Boden is widely published in poetry magazines and anthologies. She also collaborates with visual artists to make place-specific text, and responsive poems that feature in pamphlets and artists' books.

She is author of articles on subjects including: health education & walking, 18th–19th century poetry, travel writing & autobiography, women's poetry, and late 20th century Scottish culture.

An independent Literature professional, she works across a broad range of educational, cultural, community and environmental settings. She blogs at helenbodenliteraryarts.wordpress.com and tweets as @bodHelen

Acknowledgements

Some of these poems have been previously published
and I would like to thank the editors of:

Antiphon—'Calder-Hebble Navigation'
Butcher's Dog—'Haar, St Michael & All Angels'
Dangerous Women Project—'Eardley'
Edinburgh Art Festival—'Signalling Art, Not War'
Far-Off Places—'Fluent'
Gutter—'Sign'
Ink, Sweat & Tears—'Valley Town'; Empties'
Mslexia—'Migrant'
National Galleries Scotland—'Design'
Neu Boots & Pantisocracies—'Remain Moon'
New Writing Scotland—'In Suburbia (iii)'
Northwords Now—'Castlebay'; 'Kinlochbervie'; 'Young Mortality'
The Blue Nib—'Emley Moor'; 'Sheds'
The Interpreter's House—'The Play's the Thing'
Shoreline of Infinity—'Asylum'; 'Edge of Edinburgh'
Spring Fling / Wigtown Book Festival—'Young Buck'
Southlight—'From an Upper Window'; 'Not the Territory'
Valley Press—'The Gallery Tour Pauses in Front of Simon
          Armitage's Portrait'

My deep gratitude to members of all the poetry communities in
which I have arrived; to all my teachers—including many I have,
nominally, taught. To all my companions on the walk.

A NOTE ON THE TYPES

The main text of this book is typeset in the American
type designer Sumner Stone's 'green' typeface, Stone Print,
green because it is very economic in use and takes less
space in extended texts than other types. It is
also, however, a beautiful serif for other uses, including
poetry. Poem titles, epigraphs and notes are set
in Sumner Stone's Stone Serif, an earlier typeface from
this renowned type designer.